UNLOCK YOUR VALUE?

About The Author

Prabhpreet Singh Lamba, a 17-year-old student from Punjab, India writes the book 'UNLOCK YOUR VALUE' for the first time. He is currently studying in a school. Writing has always been one of his hobbies, and he always wanted to share his ideas with others through a book. This book is the result of his efforts to inspire others to become valuable in their lives. As a student, he has faced many challenges and has learned many valuable lessons that he wants to share with the world. With this book, he hopes to motivate and encourage others to pursue their dreams and become the best version of themselves.

UNLOCK YOUR VALUE?

CONTENTS

Preface   1

Introduction   3

PART-1
PERSONAL DEVELOPMENT

Defining Value	6
The Importance of Self-Care	9
Finding Your Passion	11
Building Resilience	13
The Power of Mindset	15
Time Management	**18**

PART-2
INTERPERSONAL DEVELOPMENT

Building Relationships	22
Communicating Effectively	25
Overcoming Obstacles	28
The Art of Networking	30
Leading with Integrity	32

PART-3
MAKING A DIFFERENCE

Taking Action	36
Embracing Change	39
Giving Back	42

The End   **45**

PREFACE

Welcome to the world of self-improvement, where each page is filled with opportunities to grow and become a better version of yourself. The journey of personal development is unique for each individual, but the destination is always the same: to find true fulfillment and purpose in life.

In this book, we will explore the various aspects of self-improvement, from defining your values and finding your passions to developing your skills, building resilience, and embracing change. Our goal is to provide you with the tools, techniques, and mindset needed to become a valuable asset to yourself, your community, and the world at large.

This book is for anyone who wants to lead a more fulfilling life, who wants to make a positive impact on the world, and who wants to achieve their full potential. It is for those who are tired of living a mediocre life and are ready to take action to create the life they truly desire.

We have taken great care to research and compile the most effective strategies and techniques to help you on your journey of self-improvement. We hope that you find this book informative, practical, and inspiring.

The journey of self-improvement is a lifelong process, and this book is just one step on that journey. We encourage you to take what you learn here and apply it in your life, and to never stop striving to become the best version of yourself.

Thank you for choosing this book, and we wish you all the best on your journey of becoming valuable.

INTRODUCTION

This book is divided into three parts, each of which focuses on a different aspect of becoming a valuable person. Part One, "Personal Development," provides strategies for self-improvement, including building skills, cultivating healthy habits, and developing a growth mindset. Part Two, "Interpersonal Development," explores how to create and maintain meaningful connections with others, including networking, communication, and leadership. Finally, Part Three, "Making A Real Difference," offers guidance on how to use your skills and relationships to create positive change in the world, through acts of service and philanthropy. Through these three parts, this book offers a comprehensive guide to becoming a more valuable person, both to yourself and to those around you.

UNLOCK YOUR VALUE?

PART -1

PERSONAL DEVELOPMENT

Chapter-1

Defining Value

Value is a concept that is central to our understanding of the world. We use it to describe the worth or importance of something, whether it is an object, a person, or an idea. But what does it really mean to be valuable, and how can we become more valuable ourselves?

At its core, value is a measure of usefulness. Something is valuable if it can help us to achieve our goals or meet our needs. In the context of human beings, being valuable means that we are able to contribute something meaningful to the world around us.

There are many different ways in which a person can be valuable. Some people are valuable because they possess a particular skill or talent, such as an artist or musician. Others are valuable because of their knowledge or expertise in a particular field. Still, others are valuable because of their ability to connect with and inspire others.

But what are the characteristics of truly valuable people? What sets them apart from the rest of us? The answer lies in their mindset and approach to life.

Valuable people tend to be driven by a sense of purpose. They have a clear understanding of what they want to achieve and why it is important to them. This sense of purpose gives them a direction and focus that is often lacking in those who are less valuable.

Valuable people are also self-aware. They know their own strengths and weaknesses and are able to use this knowledge to their advantage. They are constantly seeking to improve themselves and are not afraid to ask for help when they need it.

Perhaps most importantly, valuable people are driven by a sense of empathy. They are able to connect with others on a deep level and are genuinely interested in the well-being of those around them. This ability to connect with and understand others is what allows them to make a meaningful impact on the world.

So, how can we become more valuable ourselves? It starts with a mindset shift. We must begin to see ourselves as valuable and recognize the unique skills and qualities that we bring to the table. We must also be willing to put in the work to develop these skills and qualities and to seek out opportunities to use them in meaningful ways.

In the next chapter, we will explore the importance of developing skills as a key component of becoming valuable. We will examine the different types of skills that are valuable and discuss strategies for developing them. By taking this first step towards becoming more valuable, we can begin to unlock our full potential and make a meaningful impact on the world around us.

Chapter-2

The Importance of Self-Care

In today's fast-paced world, it's easy to get caught up in the hustle and bustle of everyday life. We often forget to take care of ourselves in the process. However, it's crucial to take some time out for ourselves to ensure that we can function optimally. Self-care involves taking care of our physical, emotional, and mental well-being. It means taking time out of our busy schedules to do things that make us happy and promote our well-being.

The benefits of self-care are immense. It can help reduce stress levels, boost our immune system, and improve our overall health. Self-care can help us feel more in control of our lives, boost our self-esteem, and improve our relationships with others. When we take care of ourselves, we can also be more productive, efficient, and focused.

Self-care can come in many forms. It could be taking a relaxing bath, going for a walk in nature, practicing meditation or yoga, or simply reading a book. Whatever it is that makes us feel happy and relaxed, we should make it a priority to incorporate into our daily routines.

One of the biggest barriers to self-care is guilt. We often feel guilty for taking time out for ourselves, especially when we have a lot on our plates. However, it's essential to understand that self-care is not a selfish act. It's necessary for our overall well-being and should be viewed as an investment in ourselves. We cannot give our best to others if we are not at our best.

In conclusion, taking care of ourselves is not an indulgence; it's a necessity. We must make self-care a priority in our lives to ensure that we can function optimally and be the best versions of ourselves. It's time to let go of the guilt and make self-care a non-negotiable part of our daily routine. By doing so, we can lead happier, healthier, and more fulfilling lives.

Chapter-3

Finding Your Passions

Finding your passions is crucial to becoming valuable. If you don't know what you're passionate about, you won't have the drive or motivation to succeed. Many people spend their entire lives working at a job they don't enjoy, simply because they don't know what they're passionate about. Finding your passions can lead to a fulfilling and satisfying life, both personally and professionally.

The first step in finding your passions is to take some time for self-reflection. Ask yourself what you enjoy doing, what makes you happy, and what you could see yourself doing for the rest of your life. Write down your thoughts and feelings in a journal or notebook. Consider what you were passionate about as a child or teenager, and see if those interests have evolved over time.

Next, try new things. If you've always been interested in music, take a class or try playing an instrument. If you've always been fascinated by art, try painting or drawing. Exploring new hobbies and interests can help you discover passions you never knew you had.

Once you've found your passions, incorporate them into your daily life. If you love to write, start a blog or journal. If you enjoy volunteering, find an organization that aligns with your values and start giving back. Incorporating your passions into your daily life can help you stay motivated and fulfilled, both personally and professionally.

It's important to remember that finding your passions is a process. It takes time and effort to explore new things and discover what you truly love. But once you find your passions, you'll be able to use them to guide your career and personal growth, and ultimately become a more valuable and fulfilled individual.

Chapter-4
Building Resilience

Resilience is the ability to adapt and recover from adversity. In life, we are constantly faced with challenges and setbacks that can test our limits. Building resilience is important because it helps us to bounce back from these challenges and move forward with greater strength and determination.

One of the most important steps in building resilience is to develop a positive mindset. This means learning to look at challenges as opportunities for growth, and viewing setbacks as temporary obstacles rather than insurmountable roadblocks. By embracing this mindset, we can maintain a sense of optimism and hope even in the face of adversity.

Another key aspect of building resilience is developing a strong support system. This can be achieved by building strong relationships with family, friends, and other supportive individuals who can provide encouragement and guidance during difficult times. Having a support system can help us to feel more connected and less isolated, which can be an important factor in building resilience.

In addition to these personal strategies, there are also practical steps we can take to build resilience. For example, maintaining a healthy lifestyle can help to improve our physical and emotional well-being, which in turn can increase our ability to cope with stress and adversity. This includes getting regular exercise, eating a healthy diet, and getting enough sleep.

Finally, it's important to remember that building resilience is an ongoing process that requires effort and commitment. We may face setbacks and challenges along the way, but by staying focused on our goals and maintaining a positive outlook, we can continue to grow and develop our resilience over time.

In conclusion, building resilience is a key component of personal growth and development. By adopting a positive mindset, developing a strong support system, and taking practical steps to maintain our physical and emotional well-being, we can strengthen our ability to adapt and recover from life's challenges.

CHAPTER-5

THE POWER OF MINDSET

The human mind is one of the most powerful and complex tools that we possess. The way we think, our beliefs, and attitudes can have a profound impact on our lives. This is why mindset is such an important topic when it comes to personal development. Our mindset shapes the way we view the world and ourselves. It determines our responses to challenges, failures, and setbacks. A positive and growth-oriented mindset is key to achieving success and fulfillment in life.

One of the main things to understand about mindset is that it is not fixed. It is not something that we are born with or that we are stuck with for the rest of our lives. Our mindset is something that we can change and develop over time. We can learn to adopt a more positive and growth-oriented mindset by changing our thought patterns and behaviors.

A growth mindset is one of the most powerful mindsets to have. It is characterized by the belief that we can learn and grow through effort and perseverance. People with a growth mindset are more likely to take on challenges and view failures as opportunities to learn and improve. They believe that their abilities and intelligence can be developed through hard work and dedication.

In contrast, a fixed mindset is characterized by the belief that our abilities and intelligence are fixed and cannot be changed. People with a fixed mindset are more likely to give up on challenges and view failures as a reflection of their inherent abilities. They are less likely to take risks and step outside of their comfort zones.

The good news is that we can learn to adopt a growth mindset. One of the most effective ways to do this is by challenging our limiting beliefs and replacing them with more empowering ones. This involves questioning our negative thoughts and looking for evidence to support a more positive and growth-oriented perspective.

Another important aspect of mindset is learning to manage our emotions. Our emotions can have a powerful impact on our thoughts and behaviors. Learning to regulate our emotions and cultivate a positive outlook can help us to stay focused and motivated, even in the face of challenges and setbacks.

Finally, it is important to recognize the role that our mindset plays in achieving our goals. When we have a positive and growth-oriented mindset, we are more likely to set challenging goals for ourselves and work hard to achieve them. We are also more likely to persist in the face of obstacles and setbacks.

In summary, developing a positive and growth-oriented mindset is one of the most important steps we can take towards achieving success and fulfillment in life. By challenging our limiting beliefs, managing our emotions, and focusing on our goals, we can learn to adopt a mindset that empowers us to achieve our full potential.

Chapter-6

Time Management

Time is one of our most precious resources, yet it is also one of the most finite. We all have the same 24 hours in a day, yet some people seem to accomplish so much more than others. The difference is in how they manage their time.

Effective time management means setting priorities and focusing on the most important tasks, rather than getting sidetracked by less important activities. It means using tools and strategies to make the most of the time available, and being mindful of how time is spent.

One of the most effective time management strategies is to prioritize tasks based on their importance and urgency. This means categorizing tasks as either important or unimportant, and urgent or not urgent. Tasks that are both important and urgent should be tackled first, followed by tasks that are important but not urgent. Less important tasks should be saved for later, or delegated to someone else if possible.

Another useful time management tool is to set specific goals and deadlines for tasks, and breaking larger tasks into smaller, more manageable steps. This helps to create a sense of focus and urgency, and can help to prevent procrastination.

It's also important to be mindful of time wasters, such as social media, excessive email checking, or excessive multitasking. These activities can quickly eat up valuable time, and can prevent you from accomplishing important tasks. By limiting distractions and being mindful of how time is spent, it's possible to make the most of the time available, and to achieve more in less time.

Ultimately, effective time management requires a combination of self-discipline, focus, and strategic planning. By learning to manage time effectively, it's possible to achieve more in less time, and to make the most of life's most precious resource.

›UNLOCK YOUR VALUE?

PART -2
INTERPERSONAL DEVELOPMENT

Chapter-1
Building Relationships

While developing our skills is an important component of becoming valuable, it is equally important to build strong and meaningful relationships with others. Relationships are the foundation of our personal and professional lives, and they can have a significant impact on our overall happiness and success.

The first step in building strong relationships is to be intentional about who we surround ourselves with. We should seek out individuals who share our values, interests, and goals, and who can support and challenge us to become our best selves. This may involve networking and attending events, joining social clubs or organizations, or simply reaching out to others with similar interests.

Once we have identified individuals with whom we want to build relationships, it is important to be proactive in building and maintaining those relationships. This may involve making time for regular check-ins or meetings, expressing appreciation and gratitude for their support, and offering our own support and resources when needed.

Another key component of building strong relationships is effective communication. We must be willing to listen actively, share our own thoughts and feelings in an authentic way, and respond to others with empathy and compassion. We should also be willing to give and receive constructive feedback, which can help us to grow and improve our relationships over time.

Building strong relationships also requires a certain level of vulnerability. We must be willing to share our own struggles and challenges, as well as our successes and achievements, with others. This can help to build trust and deepen our connections with those around us.

In addition to building one-on-one relationships, it is also important to build relationships with larger communities and networks. This may involve volunteering, participating in group activities or initiatives, or simply being an active and engaged member of our community. By contributing to something larger than ourselves, we can build meaningful connections and make a positive impact on the world around us.

In conclusion, building strong relationships is a critical component of becoming valuable. By being intentional about who we surround ourselves with, proactively building and maintaining relationships, communicating effectively, being vulnerable, and contributing to larger communities, we can deepen our connections with others and make a meaningful impact on the world around us. By investing in our relationships, we can unlock our full potential and create a life of purpose and fulfillment.

Chapter-2

Communicating Effectively

Effective communication is one of the most important skills we can develop in life. It is the foundation of all relationships, whether personal or professional, and can have a significant impact on our success and happiness. In this chapter, we will explore the key components of effective communication and provide strategies for improving our communication skills.

The first step in effective communication is to be an active listener. This means truly focusing on what the other person is saying, rather than just waiting for our turn to speak. We should strive to understand their point of view, acknowledge their feelings, and show empathy and understanding. This can help to build trust and deepen our relationships with others.

Another key component of effective communication is being clear and concise in our own messaging. We should strive to communicate our ideas and thoughts in a way that is easy to understand and free of unnecessary jargon or technical language. This can help to ensure that our message is received and understood by our audience.

In addition to being clear and concise, we should also be confident in our communication. This means speaking with authority and conviction, even if we are unsure of our message. We should also be willing to ask questions and seek clarification when needed, rather than assuming that we understand what the other person is saying.

Body language is also an important component of effective communication. We should strive to maintain eye contact, use appropriate gestures, and be aware of our posture and tone of voice. This can help to convey confidence and sincerity in our communication.

Another key aspect of effective communication is being adaptable and flexible. This means being able to adjust our communication style based on the needs and preferences of our audience. For example, we may need to communicate differently with a coworker than with a client or customer. By being adaptable, we can ensure that our message is received and understood by our audience.

Finally, it is important to practice effective communication on a regular basis. This may involve seeking out opportunities to speak in public, giving presentations, or simply practicing our communication skills with friends or colleagues. By consistently working to improve our communication, we can build our confidence and become more effective communicators over time.

In conclusion, effective communication is a critical component of success in both our personal and professional lives. By being an active listener, clear and concise in our messaging, confident in our communication, aware of our body language, adaptable and flexible, and practicing regularly, we can improve our communication skills and deepen our relationships with others. With effective communication, we can unlock our full potential and achieve our goals.

Chapter-3

Overcoming Obstacles

Life is full of ups and downs, and everyone faces obstacles at some point. The most successful people are those who learn to overcome these obstacles and turn them into opportunities for growth. In this chapter, we will explore the ways in which you can overcome obstacles in your life.

The first step in overcoming obstacles is to identify them. Take some time to reflect on the challenges you have faced in the past and consider the ones you are currently facing. Once you have identified the obstacles, you can start to develop a plan for overcoming them.

One of the most important things you can do is to stay positive. Negative thoughts and emotions can hold you back and make it difficult to find solutions to your problems. Try to reframe your thoughts in a more positive way and focus on the opportunities for growth that the obstacle presents.

It is also important to seek support from others. Talk to friends, family, or a mentor about the obstacles you are facing. They may be able to offer advice, provide emotional support, or connect you with resources that can help you overcome the obstacle.

Another key to overcoming obstacles is to take action. Identify the steps you need to take to overcome the obstacle and start taking action. Even small steps can make a big difference and help you build momentum.

Finally, remember to be patient and persistent. Overcoming obstacles takes time and effort, but with persistence and perseverance, you can overcome even the most challenging obstacles.

In conclusion, overcoming obstacles is a crucial skill that can help you achieve your goals and live a fulfilling life. By identifying the obstacles, staying positive, seeking support, taking action, and being patient and persistent, you can overcome any obstacle that comes your way

Chapter-4

The Art of Networking

In the professional world, networking is crucial to career success. It's not just about making connections, it's about building relationships. It's about developing trust, respect, and mutual benefit with those in your industry. Networking can lead to new job opportunities, client referrals, and valuable insights.

One of the most important aspects of networking is to be genuine. When you meet someone new, take the time to get to know them. Ask about their career, their interests, and what they're passionate about. Don't just jump into business right away. Show that you're interested in them as a person, not just as a potential contact.

Another important aspect of networking is to be proactive. Don't wait for opportunities to come to you. Attend industry events, join professional organizations, and reach out to people in your industry. Offer to buy someone coffee or lunch, and use the opportunity to get to know them better. You never know where these connections may lead.

It's also important to be professional in your networking efforts. Dress appropriately, have a polished elevator pitch, and follow up with those you meet. Be sure to thank them for their time and remind them of how you met.

One of the most valuable aspects of networking is the potential for mentorship. Seek out those in your industry who have more experience than you and ask for their guidance. Learn from their successes and failures, and apply those lessons to your own career.

In today's digital age, networking doesn't just happen in person. Social media can be a powerful tool for building professional relationships. LinkedIn is a great platform for connecting with others in your industry, and Twitter can be a useful way to stay up-to-date on industry news and trends.

Overall, networking is an art that takes time and effort to master. By being genuine, proactive, professional, and open to mentorship, you can build meaningful relationships that will help you achieve your career goals.

Chapter-5

Leading With Integrity

One of the hallmarks of a valuable individual is their ability to lead with integrity. The importance of leadership can never be overstated, as every individual at some point will find themselves in a position of leadership, be it in their personal or professional lives.

Leading with integrity is not about imposing one's will on others or forcing others to do things your way, but about setting an example through personal conduct and character. People are attracted to leaders who demonstrate moral courage and who inspire them to be better. Leading with integrity requires humility, empathy, and a deep understanding of human nature.

A valuable individual understands that true leadership is not about power, position, or authority, but about service. A leader's primary responsibility is to serve the people they lead, to help them reach their full potential and achieve their goals.

To lead with integrity, one must first develop a strong sense of self-awareness. This means understanding one's values, beliefs, and personal strengths and weaknesses. A leader who is self-aware is better equipped to make decisions that are aligned with their values and goals.

Another important aspect of leading with integrity is the ability to communicate effectively. A leader who can clearly and persuasively articulate their vision and goals is more likely to inspire and motivate others. Effective communication also involves active listening, which allows the leader to understand the needs and concerns of the people they lead.

Leading with integrity also means being accountable and taking responsibility for one's actions. A valuable leader understands that they are not infallible, and they are willing to admit their mistakes and learn from them. They also understand the importance of recognizing the contributions of others and giving credit where it is due.

Finally, a valuable leader is committed to continuous learning and personal growth. They are always seeking new ways to improve themselves and their leadership abilities, and they are not afraid to seek feedback from others.

In summary, leading with integrity is about serving others, communicating effectively, being accountable, and committing to personal growth. A valuable individual understands that true leadership is not about power or authority, but about setting an example through personal conduct and character. Through their actions and their words, they inspire others to be the best that they can be.

In conclusion, building strong relationships is a critical component of becoming valuable. By being intentional about who we surround ourselves with, proactively building and maintaining relationships, communicating effectively, being vulnerable, and contributing to larger communities, we can deepen our connections with others and make a meaningful impact on the world around us. By investing in our relationships, we can unlock our full potential and create a life of purpose and fulfillment.

Part -3
Making A Real Difference

Chapter-1

Taking Action

Taking action is one of the most important steps we can take in achieving our goals and living a fulfilling life. While it can be easy to get stuck in a cycle of planning and dreaming, it is only through taking action that we can turn our dreams into reality. In this chapter, we will explore the key components of taking action and provide strategies for overcoming common obstacles that can prevent us from taking action.

The first step in taking action is to define our goals and create a plan for achieving them. This may involve setting specific, measurable, achievable, relevant, and time-bound (SMART) goals and breaking them down into actionable steps. We should also be willing to adjust our plan as needed and remain flexible in the face of challenges or setbacks.

Another key component of taking action is to prioritize our goals and focus our time and energy on the most important tasks. This may involve setting aside distractions and learning to say no to requests or commitments that are not aligned with our priorities. By staying focused on our goals, we can avoid getting sidetracked and make meaningful progress towards achieving them.

Fear and self-doubt are common obstacles that can prevent us from taking action. To overcome these obstacles, we should be willing to take risks and step outside of our comfort zones. We should also cultivate a growth mindset, embracing failures and setbacks as opportunities for learning and growth. By pushing past our fears and doubts, we can develop resilience and build confidence in our abilities.

Another key component of taking action is to build accountability and support into our lives. This may involve seeking out mentors, coaches, or accountability partners who can provide guidance, feedback, and support. We should also be willing to ask for help when needed and lean on our support network for encouragement and motivation.

Finally, it is important to take care of ourselves and prioritize self-care in our lives. This may involve setting boundaries, taking breaks when needed, and engaging in activities that promote physical and mental well-being. By taking care of ourselves, we can maintain the energy and motivation needed to take action and achieve our goals.

In conclusion, taking action is an essential component of achieving our goals and living a fulfilling life. By defining our goals, prioritizing our time and energy, overcoming fear and self-doubt, building accountability and support, and prioritizing self-care, we can develop the resilience and motivation needed to take action and make our dreams a reality. With consistent effort and commitment, we can unlock our full potential and create a life of purpose and meaning.

Chapter-2

Embracing Change

Change is an inevitable part of life, and learning to embrace it is a valuable skill. Many people are afraid of change, preferring to stay in their comfort zones rather than take risks and face the unknown. But change can bring new opportunities, growth, and success. In this chapter, we will explore the importance of embracing change and how to do it.

To begin, it is important to recognize that change can be difficult, and it is natural to feel apprehensive about it. However, by reframing our thinking and seeing change as an opportunity rather than a threat, we can approach it with a more positive attitude. This can lead to a more open-minded approach to change and a willingness to take risks.

One of the keys to embracing change is to be proactive rather than reactive. Instead of waiting for change to happen to us, we can take control of the situation and actively seek out opportunities for growth and change. This might mean taking on new challenges at work, pursuing a new hobby, or taking a course to learn a new skill.

It is also important to be adaptable and flexible in the face of change. This means being open to new ideas, approaches, and ways of doing things. Rather than clinging to old habits or routines, we can learn to adapt and adjust to new situations.

Another important aspect of embracing change is learning to let go of the past. This might mean letting go of old relationships, beliefs, or habits that no longer serve us. By letting go, we create space for new experiences and opportunities to come into our lives.

Finally, it is important to cultivate a growth mindset when it comes to change. This means seeing every challenge or obstacle as an opportunity to learn and grow. Rather than seeing failure as a sign of weakness or incompetence, we can see it as a chance to learn and improve.

In conclusion, embracing change is a crucial skill for success and personal growth. By reframing our thinking, being proactive, adaptable, and flexible, letting go of the past, and cultivating a growth mindset, we can learn to embrace change and thrive in an ever-changing world.

Chapter-3

Giving Back

Giving back to others is an important aspect of becoming valuable. It allows us to connect with others, make a positive impact on the world, and experience a sense of fulfillment and purpose. In this chapter, we will explore the many ways in which we can give back and make a difference in the world.

One of the most obvious ways to give back is through volunteer work. By donating our time and skills to organizations and causes we care about, we can make a direct impact on the lives of others. This might involve volunteering at a local charity, participating in community service projects, or offering our expertise to a nonprofit organization.

Another way to give back is through charitable donations. By contributing money to organizations and causes we believe in, we can support their mission and help to make a difference in the world. This might involve donating to a specific charity, supporting a crowdfunding campaign, or participating in a fundraiser.

We can also give back by using our talents and skills to help others. This might involve mentoring a young person, offering pro bono services to a nonprofit organization, or using our professional expertise to help solve a social issue. By sharing our talents with others, we can make a tangible impact on the world and inspire others to do the same.

In addition to these more traditional ways of giving back, there are many other creative ways to make a difference in the world. For example, we might start a community garden, organize a book drive, or start a social media campaign to raise awareness about a specific issue. By thinking outside the box and using our creativity, we can make a positive impact in our communities and beyond.

Finally, it is important to remember that giving back is not just about making a difference in the lives of others. It is also about our own personal growth and fulfillment. By giving back, we can develop a sense of purpose, build meaningful relationships, and experience a greater sense of connection to the world around us.

In conclusion, giving back is an essential part of becoming valuable. By volunteering, donating, using our talents and skills, and thinking creatively, we can make a positive impact on the world and experience a greater sense of purpose and fulfillment in our own lives.

THE END

The book, "UNLOCK YOUR VALUE," aims to guide readers on the journey of becoming a more valuable person in every aspect of their life. It covers a wide range of topics including developing the right mindset, cultivating key traits and habits, building strong relationships, communicating effectively, taking action towards goals, embracing change, and giving back to the world. The book provides practical strategies and tools for personal growth, career advancement, and a more meaningful life. By adopting the principles and strategies outlined in the book, readers can achieve their goals and create a fulfilling and meaningful life.

UNLOCK YOUR VALUE?

NOTES

UNLOCK YOUR VALUE?

UNLOCK YOUR VALUE?

UNLOCK YOUR VALUE?

www.ingramcontent.com/pod-product-compliance
Lightning Source LLC
LaVergne TN
LVHW041555070526
838199LV00046B/1983